TRUSTING ICE

TRUSTING ICE

PEGGY O'BRIEN

•

Orchises Washington 2015

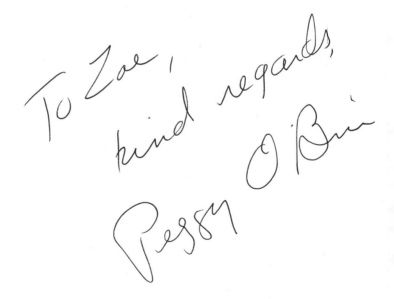

To Zoe,
kind regards,
Peggy O'Brien

O'Brien, Peggy, 1945-
[Poems. Selections]
Trusting ice / Peggy O'Brien.
    pages ; cm
ISBN 978-1-932535-33-4 (alk. paper)
1. Ireland—Poetry I. Title.
PS3615.B763A6 2015
811'.6--dc23
                                        2014017827

ACKNOWLEDGMENTS

The following poems, sometimes in a slightly different form, appeared in the following publications:"High" in *The Stinging Fly;* "Stripped" and "The Hanging" from the sequence, "Tobacco," in *The Bend;* "Crustaceans" in *The New Yorker;* The Lighthouses of Dublin Bay" in *The Irish Times;* the sequence "Monhegan" in *The Common*; and "Tracking in Winter" in *The Yale Review.* "Permission to Burn" from the sequence, "Neighbors," appeared in the book, *Maintaining a Place: Conditions of Metaphor in Modern American Literature.*

COVER: detail from *Enjoying the Ice near a Town,* Hendrick Avercamp, c. 1620; Rijksmuseum, Amesterdam.

ORCHISES PRESS
P. O. BOX 320533
ALEXANDRIA, VA 22320-4533

G 6 E 4 C 2 A

for my husband,

WYNN ABRANOVIC

TABLE OF CONTENTS

TRUSTING ICE

Night School

My lessons with him began
not with the *basso profundo*
of bullfrogs in camouflage,

or the eerie double exposure
of deer at dawn or dusk,
less animal than apparition.

It was obvious and subtle,
all about texture, tone,
a grease stain on gabardine,

a casual remark with edge.
The day had been titanium.
The night put on cast iron

clothes. We dressed as thieves —
dark jackets, pants and gloves,
caps pulled down, scarves up,

mouths taped. No cues, not even
an arched, eloquent eyebrow,
my usual, gentle learning

curve. Just eyes with cross-hairs,
sights we'd squint down and then
shoot like paparazzi

our dull, workaday quarry
due any minute now,
to punch in for the night shift.

Standing on a stripped bank,
looking out over shivering water,
shifting from foot to foot,

I wanted to scream, "Take me
home. I need to sip Merlot,
melt garlic over a low flame,"

not stare into the glassy
void willing it to grow
cute fur, warm flesh now,

eyeball drill an impenetrable
mud and wattle, cranial
dome in the middle of nowhere.

I needed to ask that practical
man what those guys
did in there…TV? Poker? Darts?

But I was emphatically not
to betray myself in any way.
I was muffled up in rules

like a kid going out to play
in theory. I began to itch,
scratch, jerk, rebel somatic,

then got what I was looking for,
a paddle, cleaver, splat
flat on water slap

in the face. I saw it coming,
the Brylcreemed, wet cat, flashbulb
popping point of it,

Castor Canadensis,
but only when I saw it
going, as the slightest thought

of loss can lend a heft
to now, that V in its wake,
which kept on as it keeps on

widening like the universe
itself, like humble twigs
of words —What were they? —when it

finally occurred, "Love is
patient," builds by stealth
and skill a dam to bursting.

Quabbin

If only we could save them
from melting, dry and press them
in some heavy book,

I'd keep that day, our hike
in late November, the start
of winter, the first snowflakes.

As a baby, when it's ready
to be born, tucks
a rosebud chin, then drops

into position, the seasons
give us ample warning
of a turn, that our planet

with its tilted, listening
face is leaning out
from that too intense light

or into it, summer,
when the slightest touch or eye
contact feels like kindness

to a cur. We smell
danger, need to hibernate,
go back into the dark

we trust, cowled Decembers
long ago when we
would make lace faces,

press them to the frosty
glass, then wait and wait
for the tightly folded child

to drop into our lap
and slowly like a plump
cloud unfold a flesh

we had to kiss and kiss,
as those flirtatious flurries,
winter's foreplay, kissed

me all over my face,
all of me I dared expose
in such weather, the snow

melting the moment it touched
the water's skin, drowned
in a reservoir of rote echoes.

The sky by then was slate,
the snow chalk, drawing fine,
radiating lines all over it,

the penetrating words an angel
speaks about a rare
flowering within a virgin.

We hadn't touched as yet.
I looked at you in profile.
In the corner of your mouth,

where smiles begin, your lips
parted showing three
white teeth. I prayed, "let it snow."

Lazarus

Silent as time it laps the sill,
Buries us beneath a pillow.
How on earth do we fight snow,
Disinter a smothered will?

New Terrain

When to trust?
By then the sun was ice.

It had to be that hard
for us to even think
of going there,
a new terrain,
where water had been
water, an element to drown in.

For weeks, we'd monitored its progress
from transparent to translucent to opaque
like scar tissue.

Enamel ripples don't let go
of anything, a too brief kiss
on the cheek, a hand
withdrawn, the smallest insult
wind inflicts, flash freeze it
to a grudge

so hard we had to risk
the swamp's interior,
or never know that maze
of tangled, sweaty hair,
gone stiff just being near
the minotaur
of choice.

inert in quartz
formaldehyde, dead
leaves, dried veins,

still sapping ramifications,
stray scraps of fern,
green filigree of summer
rusting under glass.

We got down on our knees to inspect
twigs ripped out of context,
seeds like tears, plump lips,
engorged ticks
going about their business
then specimens in amber.

We each brought sticks
to tap the unseen, sound the unsaid,

both refused
to budge,
until we got a solid
lack of echo back.
(If it rings like a too sweet
bell, he warned,
it's hollow.)

So it went,
touch and go
we made our way
by baby steps
across a surface that proved
strong enough to hold
the weight of our seasoned indecision,

knowing ice
can clear

its throat, crack
its knuckles, break up altogether
fast, like that,
not the way to learn
your lesson, stop
getting ahead
of yourself,
forgetting how slick
it is underfoot,

forgetting it's the tension
that makes ice ice,
keeps it from slipping
through your fingers.

Tracking in Winter

We walk and someone follows,
Each hoof a cloven nib,
Our testament in snow,
The snow a linen bib,
Fingers and a thumb,
Impressionable bread,
There's hunger in the tomb
Following the dead.

I've been known to crawl
To go where I have to go,
Under or over a fallen
Log, cravenly to follow,
Stay on the scent of it,
Whatever it is
Under my skin. I cannot
Sink too low. Bliss
Not making the decisions —
East or west, up
Or down, not being riven
By each leaden step,

The calligraphy of pine
Needles, against the blank
Of morning, randomly aligned,
Drafting paper, ink.
To stoop and study these prints
Is to live in the Southern Song
Dynasty, the artist sprinting
Across ice, each stroke a gong.

This must be a rabbit,
Ellipsis on the hop —
Dot, dot, dot, dot, dot, dot —
Padding every step.
The dithering of sparrows,
Every-which-way doubts,
The teardrop path of sorrow,
Squeaks, a harmless mouse,
Medieval abbot turkeys,
Illumination, iron
Claws, objective exegesis
Vulgate pristine Latin.

Some depart mid-sentence,
Words, a sense of purpose
Gone, white, dumb expanse.
It walked like us, then rose,
Continues to grow darker
As the facts grow clear,
As they do here. We mark
The spot, pronounce it murder,
Rumpled snow, a scuffle,
Still bleeding drops of blood,
Animals track animals
Followed by the dead.

Epiphany

"Have you heard?" he chirped
From the thicket of his paper.
"The birds are back." "I have,"
I whistled from a bulb-lit kitchen

Stirring a pot of old snow
Porridge. I had but hadn't
Flown there yet, dared
Utter an unfledged word.

Falling in love, from body
To mind and back again,
Landing on one, particular
Branch and singing to the dawn.

It did make sense, all right.
The crow black mornings
Rustling lacquer feathers
Earlier and earlier these days.

My beak turned toward a window,
Lethal seeking proof
Within reflective glass,
Colliding with yourself,

Failing to see far-seeing
Magi eyes, metal rays
Drilling through January,
A woodpecker at deadwood.

This Winter

Less snow, more ice,
It's been a lesson
About malice.

We need the sun,
The healing poultice
Of compassion.

Rough Justice

Not to worry. Just
A mouse, scrounging, scraping
By on others' crusts.

Night is furtive, furry,
Darting dreams. We do
Outlandish deeds, then vanish.

Hung for a poacher, just
A humble gleaner taking
For gold what's chaff to us.

Going about our business,
Mindless wind-up toys.
Then what was that? Kaput.

Insisting it was just
A mouse, I'm caught between
My scruples and my toast.

Too Fast

The frozen time between the sun and moon,
When it gets faster than ever. The one last run,
The one after that, on and on, no end
In sight, sliding at twilight, the wet snow glass,
Your pious, balking sled, a daredevil hurtling
Headlong, headfirst, hell-bent down, your two
Satanic runners steeled to deliver you straight
To the bottom, body and soul in one piece.

But not so fast. First you had to suffer
And survive the glare ice bumps and ruts,
Whip up like the ghost of a flour sack, flop back,
A dead fish slap against the only fact
To trust, that shuddering sled, the rush of adrenalin,
Catastrophe back there the near miss up ahead.
You're nothing but the track you leave behind,
Parallel lines a jet chalks on the sky.

When did I start gliding to a standstill
On a cloud? When did it get dark?
I can hear the kids still at it on the hill,
Feel the cut of acid crystals on my skin,
The prick of stubble like my father's beard
(Hair perseveres, keeps growing in the grave),
My mother's voice skating across a great
Distance, "supper," she shouts, calling me home.

January Sunset

Too soon for the coffin,
Minutes tightening the screws,
Such blood it can't be true
The sun will rise again.

High

No plan, no destination, jump in the car,
Reverse, keep reversing back to March.

Stay close to water, the path of least
Resistance, freed, going downhill fast,

Up to where there's still an ocean
Of snow in the woods, no squeak of brown.

So steep, you shift into low gear,
Wind the clock all the way back to winters

So severe they burned like dry ice,
Deep-piled drifts, an Alpine loss.

You'd begun to lose your balance. Things
Had begun to heat up, slip, tip into spring.

You didn't know you needed elevation,
A few illicit hours right at the fulcrum

Between seasons. Bulbs poking their noses,
Murky matters best left unexposed.

You were driven to go up to Worthington,
To stand and stain a pristine common,

Curse from a height, that white steeple,
Built by the most upstanding people,

They drove a stake in Heaven's face,
Made the earth spin like a mad compass,

Placed on top a crowing cock,
The so and sos, wind devout, pragmatic.

You can have your cake and eat it too
On the full circle plate of a high meadow,

The birches are still easily erased,
A pencil sketch, the page still chaste,

A hawk inflected quiet, not
The racket down below, leaves in rut.

Inside their church, you still can hear
Dust fall, but run a gauntlet to get there.

Spent, grey maples, arthritic in prayer,
Sap anathema, like breath to a martyr.

Back home, their daughters bleed, are young
Mothers, a kid on each hip, bucket hung.

The ballast to stay put, a mere moth,
A great love, so long as it weighs enough.

Spring Cleaning

The sun is shining like it means it.
Mistress March is on a tear.
The wind is her broom and she is sweeping
Up the litter left by February,

January and December misdemeanors,
Sand and grit, but they add up,
Our sly tricks to make the slippery safe,
Getting from here to there and back.

Then there's the slight problem of the fallen
Limbs and leaves. The yard is a battlefield
After the fray. Corpses strewn,
The remaining pyres of snow smoking.

The fist of ice lets go its grip
And we get to see what's been trapped
In it, start to hear the melting
Rush of promise sprinting downhill,

Laundry day when it was Mondays
And things enjoyed impeccable order,
Evil slapped and beaten out,
Scum and suds, sucked down the drain.

All it took was this little bit of kind,
Reliable light to make me see
How reprehensible my windows are.
And to think I called this dimness winter.

The Leatherman

March 5, 2011, *The New York Times*, Ossining, New York: *As the snow*
begins to recede from the meager headstone with the wrong name on
its bronze plaque, this is the question being asked about the homeless
wanderer, dressed in a 60-pound leather suit, who died more than a
century ago. How best to remember a man who spent his life, it seems,
intent on being unknown?

Why not exhume a man who never gave
his name, unscrew his secrets, pry the lid,
extract with forceps answers from the dead?
Who are you? Where are you from? Why do you live

like an animal, a base Neanderthal, snarling,
growling, baring your fangs, scrounging for windfalls,
hibernating winters, summers too exposed,
buck naked under a lean-to leaking stars?

By God, they'll make his ashes talk. Walk
a mile in another man's shoes, we say. Forget
the clichés. They're worn as the soles of the old boots
they'd abandon and he'd redeem, releasing

their butterfly uppers, stitching one to the other
tight as the pelts in a rich man's fur, or
the feuding, flattened lobes of too many
brains sutured with catgut, trying to keep it

together, that tough, taciturn, second skin
he'd don each morning to perform one part
of his annual circuit: three-hundred and sixty-five miles,
his generous tithe to the calendar and clock church.

He'd spot a familiar silo or steeple, tear off
a page, then glue it back, spotting those two,
locked limbs still circling the prison yard,
black numbers telling the sun to rise and set.

To those who live on a flat planet, it's May.
To him, it's time to cavort in a shaded dell
with buxom lady slippers. He hasn't seen or felt
himself like this since all the trees were on fire.

Today the sun can't bear to be alone.
The bashful "leatherman" bathes his flesh lovingly
as the flayed and gutted carcass of a deer,
splashing water under folds, letting it seep

into cracks. He trusts the river not to blurt
what happened up there—blizzard after blizzard,
unendurable weight straining his beams.
He tried to stop it but it came like a burst

of robins from a tangled skein of hawthorn.
The ice gave way, a deep-down rush and roar,
taut quiet on top, a pot about to break
into a boil: Bedlam, maelstroms, spring.

Clean again, anonymous as pollen,
he ambles back grazing on wild morels.
The moon, more kin than friend, wary of giving
it all in a flash, is full on this mild night

without a hint of wind. It's safe to sleep
in his God-given skin. The archer, bear and twins
each in their place. Shy, wide, ember eyes
closing in, nothing more sinister than hunger.

Lady Luck

Blowsy apple blossoms,
Drifts of ermine, wind.
I hardly know the season
Outside the grand salon.

Spinning like a whirligig.
There isn't time to grieve,
Even the trees are dizzy,
When luck is in the air.

I'd gladly squander all
the gold of every mogul
daffodil on earth
to own one penny of pollen.

All the legendary beauties,
Viburnum, lilac, lily
Of the valley have arrived.
It's so unfair. They're girls

Again, though like old ladies
Tart it up, wear far too much
Perfume. It costs the earth
And reeks on them of heaven.

One slender flower extends
An arm, prepares to make
The weather turn for good.
Heliotropic heads swivel,

Petals roll like hail,
Like pearls. The dice stop dead,
Eye us each square in the face.
The house always wins.

Neighbors

To Ron and Breda Callan

1. Permission to Burn

Like a parenthesis,
a small, walled garden
in the midst of verbiage,

there's this pause in the tedious
thicket at the back,
that leads like an afternoon nap

to pure sweetness, a couple
so close they seem bound
by morning glory vines.

When the weather turns, we turn
to pruning back last summer,
making room for this

spring. That deer run lets us
each leap over and back,
nibble and chat, nothing

serious, until like an army
in alarming scarlet tunics
the fire truck arrives.

Since we're grateful to live
in this careful town, we're careful
to seek permission to burn,

be assured we can contain it.
When the sun becomes a plausible
enough savior, there's this need

for a purge, some small punctuation
between seasons. Asperging
pine boughs brisk the air

as the congregation gathers,
refugees from behind
enemy lines. Word spreads

like the thaw. Neighbors melt
from the frozen woods, trailing
their litters of fanning saplings.

It all comes out around
the fire, the ordeal of winter,
saga of the siege,

gossip first like kindling,
finally, hoary, fallen
limbs, losses that require

flame, exorcising fever,
flailing, ululating, shrill
wailing, choking smoke.

We step back, form a fire
wall of flesh, grant all
consuming grief its season.

2. Wisteria

May again, procreation,
an almost too sweet lilac
nuzzling a grizzled barn,

that grey the grey of ashes
strewn like gritty seeds
under your Magnolia.

Right now, up in Pelham
in that graveyard deep
in woods, which once were fields,

the bumptious, new moss
is springier than ever.
Leaves chatter like teenagers,

while the terse farmers
at their feet, who cleared
the incorrigible forest,

hefted endless burdens,
walls that still contain them
under stones that tell us

when they left, April,
May, so often spring,
the flayed earth honest

at last, dying of relief
or more, are mute. Stare
into snow long enough and

the heart stops blind.
We get exhausted living
in this inexhaustible womb.

Even men in the end
sprout paps, the pendulous blossoms
of that vine, which comes back

every year, wisteria,
ghosting your porch, Maria,
that grande dame lavender

you'll never live to wear.
I can hear the toddler grass
having a tantrum the day

you made your decision, see
your breath on glass, realize
the crystalline completion of frost.

3. Fiddling

Like the late afternoon violence
we've come to depend on daily
to clear the air, but that

requires the whole orchestra
and this is strictly solo.
You also hardly hear it

at first. It's like tasting
honey or brandy and finding
you've swallowed the sun whole.

Also, this occurs after
Supper. The dishes are done,
the floor is swept, a space

some would fill with the one
cigarette, sit on the porch
and watch the smoke expand.

Only she stands straight as a tree,
neck crooked like a heron,
and begins to play her violin.

It's a long way from autumn,
a thunder clap but not,
more drawn out bone by bone,

twig snapping in the slow
split seconds after a fall.
It shook our every sill.

I sat bolt upright, got up,
looked around, saw nothing
amiss, then went back up,

sank into a feather bed
of neighborly collusion,
trusting morning to tell all.

Now it's sticky, bickering August,
fireflies falling in
and out of total love

in the meadow below the window
where I sit and fiddle
in my way, trying to make sense

of stable lighthouses adrift,
at sea, when the dusk is smooth,
calm as the pond at dawn.

There's even a protruding
moon, the belly button stem
of ripe, high, full-term summer.

Only later do I finger
the beam, resin the bow,
back to the source, consider

the past year, twin spires,
two spruce, in dark green uniform,
flanked their church-white house,

until that night when one
toppled from as little force,
apparently, as a goodbye kiss.

4. At the Helm

The problem was erosion:
the acute slope dividing
our property from theirs.

The solution was to share
the cost of having a
retaining wall constructed.

Tight as a mast sunk
into the rib cage of
a clipper it would fit

into the bank like Eve
into Adam's corrupt flesh,
keep the line between us

straight. That was the deal:
we'd get extra land,
they the pleasure of a work

of art to gaze at daily,
a grey mosaic, magic
of random fragments fitting

as if pre-determined.
A single genome marries
another and you are you.

Artisans adept as Noah,
cubit by cubit obeying
Yahweh, lay those flat slabs

course after course, dry
stacking to ensure drainage,
tamping, chinking, checking

for wobble, keeping the whole thing
level, finding the exact
balance like good neighbors,

spats and feasts and silences,
famished plants watered
for each other, the extra set

of keys kept in the cupboard,
never used, unless
requested, a reserve of trust,

money under the mattress.
So it went, Genesis,
including the flood. The wall

was the least but the beginning
of our woes. Our black
walnut trees with their alien

palm leaves so far north,
waved goodbye, as the very
peaks from which the rock

was plundered drowned and we
were marooned, each in their ark,
Mr. and Mrs. Noah,

immured with all those beasts,
creeping, crawling, clean,
unclean, writhing, seething

iron shells packed tight
with maggots, loose, licentious,
swarming, non-stop spawning.

In the end it wouldn't matter
whether the raven or
the dove came back, or even

whether that harbinger of peace
returned again and again
winging green hope in its beak.

One day it was bound
to go for good, drop
beneath the always provisional,

final line that keeps
on slipping through our fingers
like all the waters' wrath.

Turtle Time

It's my discipline to walk
and the older, stiffer I get
the more I demand the straight line
of a child's exercise book,

this defunct railway track,
where flashing yardsticks once
clocked the sleepy inches
speeding by as miles.

I need the neat contrast:
left and right, then
and now, cost and profit,
peripatetic trade-offs.

On the one hand, this field
scorched black, a postage stamp
from hell. They must have lit
the perimeter, then let it rip.

Think of the strain, holding
a wet, solitary finger,
Lear on the heath, up
to the ever changing wind.

Feel the flaying heat,
when smolder flips to flare,
sucks our every precaution
into its orange maw,

then levitates as smoke.
Regard that square of char
as all in a day's work
and keep on floating.

Only then will you be set
to feel each needle spear
your threadbare flesh, begin
weaving new linen skin,

a green that was never greener,
a mop of hay never thicker,
rejuvenating magic
this flirting with fire.

On the other hand, that swamp,
clutter, scum, bubbles, burps,
twenty-four-seven hatching,
wriggling, croaking, rot.

Couch potato turtles
on a log. If the sun stays
out, they'll stay there
warming their reptile blood.

They don't even risk sunburn
under their umbrellas,
boil or simmer, even milder
melt, except perhaps into

each other, seniors in chairs,
a row of dominoes collapsed,
old flames or rivals honed
to serene, overlapping ovals,

no lines or angles, Buddha
smooth within their shells,
the family jewels, passed on
through generations, strata,

epics, eons, glacial
slowness and compression,
freezing heat: revolutions
won and lost in turtle time.

Going, they're on my right
coming back, my left.
By late afternoon, they glow
like lustrous lumps of anthracite.

Cat Tails

Rhizomes growing out not down in time,
Shunning deep attachment, needing air.
You're the statistician. Just how random
Was it? You and me. Dandelion fluff,
Willy-nilly drifting everywhere, seed,
Mad vagaries of wind, the sure tug of gravity.

I'd just become a grandmother, acquired gravity,
I thought, taken root in a spring meadow. Time
Was a door blown open by the wind. One seed
Became my sun, my gleaming girl. The air
Was gold between my teeth, that solid. Fluff
Turned flesh, ten fingers, toes, hardly random.

No discernible pattern. Please, I know random.
My all too predictable bids to defy gravity,
Helpless sperm word rants, shotgun fluff,
An invading, khaki cat tail army. Time,
Says the muskrat, for my pleasure. I will air
An anger rampant as fire then run to seed.

So quiet in the woods we're each a seed
Tied to the fine filament of breath. Random
Thoughts, regular breathing, in and out of air,
Waxy silence, incremental gravity.
Love ricochets off logic until time
Bursts its calloused pod, lets fly infinite fluff.

When words fly back into your face, fluff
Frustration, sit tight in your rib cage, be a seed
In a winter swamp, a frozen maze, let time
Slip and slide you, loose the knot, random,

Wandering ways. You'll find your center of gravity
Again, find yourself walking on water, air.

We rubbed one against the other. The air
Grew goose bumps, blinded and bedazzled us with fluff.
Young love, late middle age, acrobatics, gravity.
The man in the moon kicks up some dust, seed
Money for a far-flung cosmic project, random
Hunch paying and paying in Croesus time.

Each star's a seed sown in the midnight air,
In time the sky starts coming down with fluff.
Our polestar isn't random. We need gravity.

Turkey Call

I check it yet again. I need to hear
From the din out there something, anything other
Than the death rattle of a star, vital words.
I press a button, get the doomed, organ sound
Of hope booting up. I'd lift a phone but who
To call? Who delivers all or nothing?

It's always been like this. Absolutely nothing,
Zilch, no one to turn to, and I hear
The stars moan like love-lorn whales. Who
Can answer that appeal except some other
Endangered creature? I like to think that sound
Is heard, someone, something finds the words.

Speed dial, memory dial, use your finger. Words.
Again and again. You keep trying. Nothing.
Sorry. Please leave a message at the sound
Of the bleeping beep. I cough, sweat, bleed, blather, hear
Myself blubbering, blush, resolve to be other
Than me, someone with the answers. Who?

Once upon a time a woman asked "Who
Is that man?" not out loud. Oh no. Words
Were not his way, unlike all the other
All-talk-big-mouths. He could say nothing
For hours, miles, then smile and she would hear
Trees falling. That's how she knew he was sound.

Courtship's different now. Sight and sound,
Skyping on a screen. But what or who
Are those eyes talking to? They appear to hear,
Get the drift, drop anchor elsewhere. Words

Fly over their interlocutor's shoulder. Nothing.
A face and a camera. When was it ever other?
An hour to turn the dial down on the other
Noise inside, start filling up with no sound.

It fits me like a silk slip with him. Nothing,
Then, I leap out of my skin. Yikes. What or who
Is that blowing on a blade of grass? Words
Scatter like scared rabbits when I hear
That bestial sound out of his mouth, then hear
Nothing, then some gobbling, proto words,
A voice on the other end enquiring, "Who?"

Tobacco

1. Landmark

Like my doubts, I counted on it being there,
All alone, a lighthouse on the flood plain in Hadley,
The middle of what had been tobacco
Country, a long, gray dilapidated shed, nearly extinct,
A dinosaur, who'd lumbered up from the Connecticut
To graze a bit and soon began to sink
Into the loam of his exhausted flesh, diminished, geriatric,
Out-to-pasture, skinny, splayed, rafters
Exposed, beams caving in. The end
Came fast, not fire nor water, wind, the mere hem of a tornado.
I heard their ire from home, the Furies howling for his bones.
They brought him to his knees,
They brought the monster down, flayed and razed a man
Who'd never stood up to a woman's anger.

2. Work

My father used to like to brag,
Though the women worked inside the barns in shade, "No daughter
Of mine is ever going on tobacco,"
Migrant pickers rubbing sweaty shoulders
With the fast girls of the town, stigmatized and stained,
Peroxide, nicotine-dyed hands, yellow
Fever, grounds for quarantine,
Not to mention, the swollen head of an unprotected thumb,
Pricked from sewing the leaves to make the sheaves swag
Like a million dollars in the gloom above them
Was another thing. One summer there was no other work.
The time had come. I knew what I needed to hear.
My father didn't demur.
He knew the value of a buck.

3. Nets

It's like being a bride again. August,
Looking through a veil, the atmosphere
So hazy it collapses distances like years. I'm back,
But still suffer
From the weather. Summer. This valley like a crotch ferments heat,
Stews it to a muggy grudge.
Every night I seek relief,
A dip or cycle through the fields to gauge
The latest progress of their progeny. Tobacco
Is back with a vengeance. Yuppie cigar aficionados.
Hadley now is tropical. Elephant ears, pachydermal
Skin, rampant like my being a teenager again
In a stifling, small New England town. I wonder when
They'll put these babies under gauze?

4. Hanging

I walked right in, the broad barn doors wide
Open, propped that way with two-by-fours, an earthen
Floor, the farmer who let me stay, provided
I agreed to ask no questions.
In through the mouth, down into the belly of the whale,
Eyes adjusting slowly to the smoky, latticed dark,
Ribs of light, tobacco speared on poles,
Bunting for the hanging, a ritual to mark
The harvest, beams at ascending levels, boys
Balancing, straddling the ties, trapeze artists
About to fly in relay, lifting their burden up with ease,
Higher and higher, priests elevating the host.
An ocean growing over my head, a dimness censed,
Leaves anointed with their own perfume, the cure commenced.

5. Minor Prophet

Joseph Kowalski is eighty-one. The skin
On his cheekbones is as smooth as an egg,
As clean a curve as the horizon
Without friends alive, except his wife and best friend, Eva.
Up at dawn every day, including the Sabbath,
After supper he wants nothing more than to sit on the verandah
With Eva or go to his workshop and hone tomorrow not advice
For upstarts. He's had his grievance with the sky.
In '38 it drowned his crop, ate a shed, staved the house in, made
      him wish
Himself dead. Now this, the anguish of being a prophet
In his own land, to tell the truth and not mete
Out the punishment. When he sees them coming up the drive to beg
For help, he's tempted to sail off in the opposite
Direction, straight across the fields, bound for Tarshish.

6. Blight

The spores of the blue mold float like rumor,
The latest person to get cancer, some misdeed,
Adultery, abuse. A good farmer looks up from his too flat,
Seven-day-a week existence, sees his neighbor, children, wife.
My father drove himself mad in his Buick careening from lawyer
To banker, managing his brother's widow's money. The road
      was narrow,
Treacherous, I know it well, twisting between greed
And duty. My father died first.
So did his putative quest for justice.
The generous tobacco leaf provides the ant with shelter. We
Divide fields, which together remain free.
By all means save your money, budget
For a catastrophic loss. At the first sign of disease, harrow
The lot, sick or not, under. You'd cut off your foot to save your life.

7. Cost

Tobacco goes now for ten bucks a pound.
Joseph Kowalski recalls when it went for sixteen cents.
Since there were times in the past when he lost his shirt and pants,
A man could easily mistake,
He admits, tobacco for God; but Joseph strives to travel light,
Packing only what he needs for one life.
He's also learned to pray just for some decent weather
Day to day, throwing overboard the luxury of fantasies
Of profit, the excessive anger certain loss
Incurs. The leaves are in the barn. They're turning brown,
Leathery as a farmer's forearm in mid-August.
Every night they close the floor-to-ceiling shutters,
Long and narrow as a lifetime in this valley. Some morning early
I'll watch them open up again, if only I can wake.

8. Stripped

An old farmhouse clad in asphalt shingles,
My father's polyester leisure suit, a chipped but opulent onion
Dome in the front garden, an angel
Fallen by a baleful wind from grace, severed forever from heaven.
Origin is myth, the silver shiver of birch leaves,
Whole forests, in even a second-generation farmer's dreams.
Broad leaf unlike shade tobacco never suffers under gauze.
It takes the sun's punishment on the chin, straight up,
Then three days and three nights, a lifetime dying, Jonah
In the barn: the hanging, curing, stripping
Of the body from the soul. Towards autumn's end a dampness seeps
Into the mornings, moisture like the merciful God weeping.
Suddenly the brittle leaves can bend again. One flick
And the spine lifts off the flesh, a fish filleted.

9. Feuds

My neighbor, Jean, a social worker, warns, "Don't romanticize
Hadley." She sees the saurian underside, the alcohol, dementia, wife
Beating, more often than not, the blight of brother
Hating brother, wars over land.
I'm as bad. I could abhor a plant for its green prosperity and health.
My father died finally of lung cancer. He never took a puff
In his life, so insidious is evil, passive
As dust most times. You should count yourself among the
            blessed,
If one day driving loose and fast, before some bystander
Is done in by your mad fuming, pacing on disputed borders,
The Lord
God himself doesn't come down, a blinding sword,
Out of the blue, splitting the murderous haze,
Demanding is your anger just?

10. Prediction

Diaries. An octogenarian farmer has kept track.
Sixty odd years of work. No personal ups and downs, the level
            facts,
Tobacco day to day: weather, fertilizers, poisons,
Pests, exact details, the sowing and the harvest, the exquisite
            process
Of the cure, scientific as mummification, all the vectors
Of success or failure, measurements and dates, mystery
            dispatched
Like the sun coming up in the east, particular
Patterns, stem-and-leaf diagrams, probability and deviation,
            statistics
From the earth, less thought than instinct
And a lot of distance from those first, slim seedlings, inklings

Only. I now accept that the plant grown here just thirty miles
      north
Of where I grew up is not the identical plant of my youth.
Other conditions, another person.
And tomorrow? Anybody's guess.

11. Summit House

Upended graves, hovering turkey vultures, the Holyoke
Range, sloping back from the Connecticut, keeping track
Of the valley below, years when the river didn't know
Where it was going, oxbowed in the doldrums.
On the first, major summit, a chalk-white, blocky structure
Rests. September mornings in the mist,
Bleached bone, a cairn. Afternoons, a glinting, distant
Wedding cake, our local Lhasa, temple of the gods.
When I'd return from a trip down river
To see my mother, threading her paranoia back
To some original sin, I'd look up and see my once flawed
Father spirited by means of sky burial finally home.
The tobacco in the Lego barns below
Is growing mellow. Our expensive anger up in smoke.

Hot Signs

Back then, he'd take me
to the compass spinning center
of the forest, let me spin
planetary in his arms,
and then, before I'd stopped,
begin
to lecture me
without one pine needle
of irony through lips like ripe
viburnum buds
on hot signs,

burning evidence
of fleet but cautious white tail near,
so near, so close
you smell smoke
streaming from the lengthy, lissome plume
they lift sirening
for cover, listening
from a distance.

Are there any oaks
around, not any oaks,
white oaks with the sweetest
nuts?

Any acorn caps
littering the ground,
incriminating bottles, crumbs, shells, seeds, shucks,
bones?

And on the margins,
where shy wilderness approaches
worldly cultivation,
near a corn field, say,
any delicately nibbled cobs?

Any awled thickets
dense as hardwood,
gas lit gallery
tunnels to or from
the master's paneled chamber
in the snow, any spoon prints
in the silk, thumb prints
on the skin?

Any bark, discarded
emery boards, worn smooth
to trim the irritating velvet
from an itchy horn?

Then come the spring
with any luck
perhaps a rococo rack
of antlers,
candelabra at a tag sale?

Bucks follow does.
Does follow fawns.
I followed him
deeper and deeper
into the arcana
of the hunt,
the *penetralia*

where men exchange their secret
we-know-
them-far-more-than-they-know-
us handshake.

Sooner or later
we'd sit on a log
and I'd dispense the edible browse
I'd packed for him,
milky, silky coffee from a bullet
flask, tender, tasty, leaf
thin, pink ham sandwiches
(the tough, too chewy
crusts cut off), Swiss
chocolate irresistible as sassafras,
apple segments tart and hard
the way he likes them.

Meanwhile, I was feasting
on the neat precision
of his eating, fingernails
like gibbous
moons,

that helpless man
unable to resist
going on and on
at table
about animals.

Any scrapes? They're like dogs,
you know, who paw the earth
to own it and then pee

on their raked patch, their pungent
urine quite the aphrodisiac.

"I see," I'd say
and still he didn't stop,
like ambivalence having sex.

Of course, the richest find of all
is droppings, recent
scat, the fresher,
the better.

"Is that so?"
I'd limply interject then
add, "I wonder
could I tempt you
with more chocolate, dear?"

To which he'd fire back,
"I thought you'd never ask."

It

It's often hard to know
not just when we're children
glued to the keyhole

exactly what they're up to.
It started paces, seconds
back. Something up

ahead, something out
of the ordinary. A complex, duplex
duck? A lazier, fatter

breed of beaver? A baby
whale inland breaching
the surface of my eyeball?

There it was, rather
there they were, rather
there we were, voyeurs

on two, huge, adult
snapping turtles, a pair
of Bose headphones, brown

crockery platters upside
down, floating, swimming
in an intricate duet.

As though on cue, they'd come
together, bang like noiseless
cymbals, then drift apart,

each pirouette, a spinning
top, then tumble as one
not on but in their water

bed. Then one would slide
onto the other's back,
and like a coin flip,

the dominance reversed.
Then being snappers there were
bites, love or hate

or both we couldn't tell.
Who can tell in the heat
of it except that it's

compelling and went on
for half an hour or so.
Then, without so much

as a by your leave, one
pushed off, swoosh, into open
water. The deed was done,

the battle won or lost.
Divorce? Who knows, even
when it's happening to them.

All I know, is the one
the author deemed abandoned
did not look desolate.

But as every reader would,
I kept waiting for the partner
to return, regret, begin

the whole flipping fugue
again, but, no, it wasn't
meant to be —she,

rather the one I'd like
to think of as me, paddled
puttered, then rolled over,

opened like a flower,
the better for the sun,
tireless, to tongue her.

Outdoor S & M

Trees, an army. I'm surrounded, stripped
Of uniform, weapons, rank. I'm read the rules.
We start to march. I'm letting myself be whipped

Into shape. He strokes my cheek, looks eagle keen,
Suggests for my own good, please, I keep my distance.
There is no talk like an angry sapling's back talk.

Everyone needs her space. Bucks rub and scrape.
Even my commander's cowlicks curl anarchic,
Refuse to be combed into place. Soldiers bivouac

Under ice pick stars, reconnoiter, sniff the air
Like wary prisoners. No choice but to suffer
The lash of love taps, smothering of kisses.

I've been through a war elsewhere. I'd speak of that
And more were it not for the barbed wire in my throat.
I'd say, "Protection for me is foreign. I fight it."

Monhegan

1. Goose Girl

I'm chatting away merrily to his back
About how my grandmother worked here
As a nursemaid. Little changes
On an island. Look, a goose girl
In a floppy bonnet, charges honking.

I follow him just as I follow
In her footsteps, leaving behind
A fist raised like a gust of wind
For the generous wingspan of an eagle,
Stillness moving, gliding silence.

2. Domesticity

As a spider anchors the threads of home
Beneath the fingernails of pinecones,
So, they say, the fairies plant themselves
In between and under roots and rocks,
Glean a life from the glut around them.

Like dewdrops in a morning glory cup
They tuck up in their bijou dwellings,
Finely balanced twigs and moss and bark.
So, the hollyhocks in town lean over
Into a neighbor's yard and talk and talk.

3. Spies

There are no large mammals on the island.
Only man. A constant chirruping
Inflates the air. Insouciant birds
Float in my hair. I'm Spring but it
Is Fall, icy fangs about to bare.

We watch and watch as though hatching
That hen and chick, clucking, pecking
In a kitchen garden, so close yet they
Refuse to flinch, looking at us
Sideways. You are a very big man.

4. Accounts

As if the miniscule but crucial
Dot on the letter i drifted
Off and landed as a self-
Sufficient island miles off from
The ruled ledger of the mainland.

A stout widower from Massachusetts
Pushed his way up into Maine,
The will-she-won't-she's of the coast,
The blank page of the ferry, all
To dot his *i*'s and cross his *t*'s.

5. Tease

A monarch butterfly, a winged
Nasturtium flirt, Salome danced
Then landed on me blurted, "Hi!
I think I know you from the Great
Atlantic Flyway. Or was it our grandmothers?

Anyway, I'm off to Mexico.
I've never been there but remember
How to go. It's time to give up
On the North, to swarm quiescent
On an Oyamel, be blossom still."

6. Exploration

When that impatient man came
On his urgent mission to ask
For her hand, did he at least pay her
The honor of exploring that island, which,
Even in her servitude, was home?

Did he get dizzy on her cliffs
(The height, the drop), lie back in her ferns,
Inspect her dappled moss, see himself
More clearly in that honest light,
Way out in the ocean, so exposed?

7. Gold

Here painters paint painters painting.
To walk is pentimento. Nothing,
Not the basest weed, is innocent
Of art. Little wonder color daubed
By no man's hand holds us in thrall.

Saffron lichen, sealing wax,
Stamped by a worn signet ring,
Branding this birch, this rock sovereign.
So one face can soften and anneal
Another. Strike a new currency.

8. Clean

When my grandfather proposed to her,
White sails puffed their cheeks, bed sheets
In a wind. Dinghies scudded. Gull wings
Ironed every doubt to certainty.
Later, she would take in laundry.

Now it's our turn, our first morning
On their island. Bleached light pours
From two directions in a corner
Room. The white, fluttery curtains
Offer little resistance to speak of.

9. Saved

The sky was a blue baptismal font,
The ocean upside down. We swam
In it. We walked and never tired,
Floated side by side on our backs,
Whenever we needed to be reborn.

Like gulls around a laden fishing
Boat, almost sinking, chugging
Into harbor, we were fully fed
And on the fly, sped with the schooner
Clouds up to the edge of a cliff.

10. Rust

Dragon's teeth, black, jagged rocks,
The bell buoy is an anxious mother,
Drop by drop, month by month,
Bleeding, bleating her warnings back
Into the salty clarity of ocean.

But a grandmother's an ivory scar
On an oyster shell, the gash long healed.
She smiles while the children clamber up
And over the giant lobster of a rusting
Hulk, paddle in the ferrous tide pools.

11. Recidivists

You can marry the same person
Again if conditions are such you can't
Resist the landscape changed but grinning
Home from ear to ear, the light
Bestowing hummingbird deep kisses.

We're fairly skipping down the aisle
From the tame side of the island to
The wild. Waxwings flit confetti.
Warblers hold my veil aloft.
All migrating to where it is hot.

12. Web

A scrub pine or a burning bush?
Depends on how you look at it.
One minute, a scrawny, naked waif
In the forest, next the chosen Christmas
Tree ablaze with blades of tinsel.

He wears a halo when he smiles,
Until his brow creases, furrows,
Cracks. The windscreen shatters. Light
Alone believes the web remains,
All those millions of resilient threads.

13. Sage

White Head. A wrinkle from a glacier,
A lookout on a sun supine sea.
We ask a hiker if we've time
To scale another height. We mean
By dark. He answers, "Life is Long."

Now, we're neither here nor there,
Ferrying back to the mainland. Our boat
Creates the waves that drown the "i"
In island. It's bitter up on deck.
I take your hand, feel everything between.

The Other Grandmother

I'd look up past an outcropping of bust,
Cornice beak and raptor eyes
To sit on the top of a snow-capped peak,

Prepare to leap into that lake
I'd heard so much about at my feet,
Something that looks exactly how

it sounds —opal, oval, open,
Lit from behind like a child's face,
Everyone and everything swims in it,

Sea and sky blue green, dawn
And dusk one blood, sun and moon,
Light and shade, an ordinary day,

My opulent, modest legacy but blank,
A wound covered with a Band-Aid.
"You can't be too careful," she'd say. Danger

Was everywhere —tuberculosis from a kiss.
Collywobbles from green apples.
Her voice became a doleful priest's,

As she'd intone her prayer to Alice,
"Alice, little Alice, my angel, "
the one grandchild who'd never erred.

Absolute doom bestowed a halo.
She'd look down on what now is mine
To protect and opine, "one crack and it's over."

Learning to Swim

We almost went to Malaga,
Cicada castanets, saffron,
Lavender, and mint, turquoise
Pool water, salty drops
Of sweat, tight swaddling of heat.

My senses were like sated leaves
Spoon-fed by the sun imagining
We five on the Mediterranean, my daughter,
Me, and her three daughters, links
In a mammalian anchor chain.

As a tree thrives leaf by thirsty leaf,
I began to believe we'd go there,
And that from our alabaster eyrie
High above the city, we'd see
Africa, the coast of its head crowning.

What is more, we'd go there too,
Ferry to Algeria, camel trek
The desert, plumb the sub-Sahara,
Push on to the boot, then bow
Before the white head of Antarctica.

By some miracle we'd reach
The pole, then go beyond it, fused
By the adventure into one
Pacific current muscling the clear,
Ancestral viscera of water,

Better still a unitary pod
Of whales, stop punishing this flesh

And celebrate its amplitude
With hymns, laments, odes and anthems,
Make the ocean's caverns echo.

Then again, it might happen where
We were, by saying the name of the region
properly —"An-duh-loo-thee-ah" —
Putting the tongue against the teeth
To check the sugar rush of fantasy,

To taste more fully every honey
Luscious vowel of now. Better
Still, it might occur right where
We are in dour, unmagical
New England at a chilly pond.

A girl will feel beneath her spine
The presence of a mother's hands.
They'll stay as long as that mimosa
Needs them there to be secure,
To feel herself alone floating.

Crustaceans

Just as I cross myself when a cat like a hearse
Cuts across my path, as though I still believed,
Before the summer goes, I'll be damned
If we don't get to the beach and eat lobster.

I dive right in waves with frosty lion manes.
It doesn't kill me to feel more alive.
Add salt to water and flesh floats higher;
Dry off in the sun and feel preserved as a cod.

Invincible, I take in hand a flailing monster,
Plunge it in a pot of boiling water,
Watch it's green copper turn to scarlet.
(Well it might, killed to appease our appetite.)

We tuck our bibs in and tuck in, yank
A claw from a socket, a swimmeret from an oarlock,
Bite and lick and suck, drool butter, devour
It before gross gluttony devours us.

It's the same Atlantic under every carapace.
We know well their bottom dwelling crevices
Between a rock and a hard place, deeper still
Burrowing denial, until the day we're trapped.

A hand trembles, the mind wobbles, one half
Wields the implements, the pick and cracker, for
The other, reeling in the kite of memory
For the first, grounding a bobbing face in a name,

Symbiosis. Love at its most evolved
Is slow, sees the life it once gulped blind.
Steroid biceps, iron pecs, antennae
To tail-fan, one tight chain of command, lightening

Reflexes. Snap. Vamoose. Get microscopic.
Inspect that tail fan, each isosceles trapezoid
Leaf eyelash-fringed with filaments of boa,
As alert as the hairs on an arm in tidal air.

Please, Poseidon, pardon us our greed,
Our need for this annual one-night stand in a cabin,
Keep the knots in the pine, the sand on the floor,
Arrest the breeze. Let us come again and again all claw.

Matinee

Bugs bungee jumping up and down,
A light switch, on and off the water's surface,
Laying eggs, perhaps, intent and helpless
As it gets. Therefore, enter a kingfisher
Dropping from the fly loft on a zip-line.

Aims, swoops, gulps in one electric arc,
Spot lit for an audience of one
This summer afternoon at Puffer's Pond,
Where all performances are live. What
Did I just see? Tragedy or comedy?

This is what it means to swim, to be
The line between seemingly opposing depths.

Flight Patterns

The mall.
Another concrete
weekend task ticked
off, no more than air. I
fly across the parking lot,
turn south for home, then stop,
hauled to the berm not by the law but by
a black magnet in the sky. I have to
watch that flock of starlings
playing with the never-
ending ways
to sculpt
a river.

Flames
and waves
and plumes of
smoke, a pixilated
lilac in a wind,
the cheetah's foetal
spots, a floating
amniotic sac,
a swarm of bees or locusts,
creatures high on living
in their own skin still
listening to the cues
emitting from
another's, skin to
nerve-end skin,
speaking
in tongues.

But elbows, ankles, knees, a shoulder
blade, the rib
cage, fingers, toes, the nose
up close, even
an eyelash can be sharp
and angular as wings designed
to cut through
nothing, plus
a couple stacked tight
all week by work can be a pair
of deckchairs un-
folding at the same time
trying to get
close.

It can take
some potent
Sabbath magic
to smooth out our
edges, time to lean
back in the tub, soak
repose up through our
pores, recreate, take direction
from what has been a remote pleasure
center, steep ourselves in spooky ordinariness,
the empty space of any blessed Sunday.

A long lie-in, sinful breakfast, fat
paper, heaping laundry
basket, grocery cart,
expensive phone
calls with our
far-flung
loved ones, pre-
parations for the day we
say will come, on to the brimming
glass, the groaning board, to sink at last
into a sofa, fade
digitalized deep into a screen.

Then on to bed,
sweet shoaling
in the sheets
praise be,
dolphin lolling, rolling,
banking, listing, meshing
atomistic every pore, each Seurat
dot against the blank a bird, a
school that doesn't need
to learn to read its larger
whence or whither,
question why we
two are one
tongue in
the mouth
of the
wind.

Remedy

My fisherman is my physician.
He knows my symptoms off by heart.
We can be walking hand-in-hand
And I am simply bound to start
Clearing my throat, picking a scab,
Popping my ears. My taciturn angler's
Bound to speak. He opens his mouth
And live syllables leap up to feed.

He cautions me to mend my line
And reassures me I know how
The current (always stronger than
It looks) drags our best cast downstream,
Bloats it tight and choked, while healthy
Hunger in our swaying depths,
Survives by staying loose, ignoring
Anything that moves unnaturally.

One quick flick corrects all that.
His tanned, flat, rock hard wrist
Mimics the flip of a leaf in the wind.
And I can see the unseen line
Respond, snake whip up, ripple all
That crippling, static tension out of it,
Floatingly, cursively coming to land,
A new language I've yet to learn.

The Lighthouses of Dublin Bay

One by one they come out,
have a thought, Cartesian
geniuses, then disappear,
fairy lights the owner
strung around a window
before leaving for vacation
in the sun.

So where do we go
from here? This rented
house sits at the top of a granite
cliff. You are solider than it.
Still, I get up
in the fœtal dark to hug
the arched belly of the bay,

wait for each in turn
to blink, philosopher stars,
trying to determine whether
or not they are —
Mugglins, Dun Laoghaire,
the Bailey, East Wall, Kish, I whisper,
a sixty-something mother-to-be.

Veteran

I thought I saw a duck,
But I was on my bike
Going fast as kids grow up.

The problem was that rear,
Big as a dinosaur egg,
A bustle made of Jell-O,

A stream-lined, duck-assed racing
Helmet, though with muscles
Twitching every which way,

Each with a will of its own,
All subject to a prior
Will, the old puzzle

Of the many and
The one, a clutch of animated
Dust balls and a mother,

So tight they might have been,
Those chicks, in egg formation,
Still inside her waiting

To be born. Soon
They'll grow and in ratio
Grow away from her,

Until they're gone, each female
At the vanguard of
Her own feisty flotilla.

The amputee feels nothing
But a phantom twinge,
Numb at the shriek of a hawk.

Rainbow Trout

I was alone all day. You were out
On the river. At twilight you came back,
Dazed and sunburned, bearing two trout

And four, new feathers, glossy black
And yellow for the kitchen table to replace
Those faded, blue ones with the lashes

Glued together like an eye that's wasted
Itself on too much grief, gone stiff,
Then dried in frayed acceptance of its loss.

So here we are. I'm washing the fish
You gutted. Then, get it, everything, the lot,
The supple rainbow and my wish.

Too Late to Swim

How I've missed you, grieved.
The recent cold spell made me
Wary, too afraid to strip off,
Dive in, swim in you.

You know how sensitive you are,
How your temperature can plunge,
Cannonball off the high
Ledge of summer, shatter

Like a sheet of ice. The rift
Was sudden. I have to be with you
Up close again. Have your leaves
changed, any new grey hairs?

I too am on the edge,
Paddling. My feet are spatulate
And white, as detached from me
As the truth of death to a child,

Who is sure summer will last
Forever, the green fountain
Of June spraying its super-
Fluity into a brimming-

Over basin of repose.
I have to talk in the non-
Linear way a leaf drifts
On your surface in the sun,

No direction, prohibitions,
Talking to the one with whom
Watching your words is not
Letting your hands wander.

Maple

The claws of an eagle,
Flying straight up,
An old sugar maple.

Clinging to a slope,
Knotted root knuckles,
Steep angle of hope.

An Elevated View

The two of us
enshrined like statues in a swan
grotto, three sides of white,
fluttering cotton, on the top floor of a sky
scraper.

For those imprisoned
in the body and who exercise inside
its shadow, the floor-to-ceiling
windows are a planned distraction.

You can jump
into the thriving city at your feet,
re-grow fins and swim
out past the islands in the harbor to the whales,
sprout wings and disappear,
a speck of dust gulped by gull grey cloud,

or just look straight down,
fall all those stories, headlong thoughts
of what might happen now —
this, that, the other, hit
bottom and bounce
back

to observe how the meandering
river also doesn't know,
as it curves past the royal
blue cupolas and gleaming spires
of Harvard, where it's going next,

or follow the riparian thread
of esplanade below, an old man
with a cane, a mother
and toddler, speed
walker, jogger, runner, roller
blader all putting
one foot unoriginally in front of
the other,

plus the unbroken flow
of bikers and the pea pod
rowers in centipede
sync going up
and down river with the easeful
quiet of a drifting stick,

not to mention
the inaudible, horn-blaring traffic
jam on suddenly short Long-
fellow bridge,
all those people, all
impatient for deliverance to the other
side.

It shouldn't matter
whose arm the needle point
of here and now punctures.

We are hooked together on an hourglass
dispensing like the bubble
vehicles on tubular
Storrow Drive below drop
after costly

monotonous
drop,
the time
the two us
have left to spend
together
here.

Triptych

1. Snakes

Weigh this and that and all of it turns circular,
Three snakes curled up into the one talisman,
My mother braiding my unruly hair.

To hiss, dart, tongue-flick, slither out of nightmare.
Medieval monks consigned them to the margins.
Weigh this and that and all of it turns circular.

Enough to drive you to the asp, the adder,
No closer to the earth, the ultimate sin,
My mother braiding my unruly hair.

That throbbing, onyx wreath, completion, summer.
Crush the viper with your heel and then?
The seasons pass in fours, the four-square years.

So easy not to see, black snakes, black tar.
Observe how the beginning bites the end,
My mother braiding my unruly hair.

Deep in its den the question is the answer,
Snakes in the sun, an old enemy your friend.
Weigh this and that and all of it turns circular,
My mother braiding my unruly hair.

2. Soap

To use the gift or hoard it in a drawer?
The secret is to cut the rose at dawn,
With always the dark undertone of cedar.

A field of color for a phial that's clear,
The allure of lather, buttermilk on skin,
To use the gift or hoard it in a drawer?

Extracting summer, pressure, slow surrender,
Oil and ash, blood and bone, the cauldron,
With always the dark undertone of cedar.

The sky at sunset, a massif of lavender,
A sachet breathing and the garden stone.
To use the gift or hoard it in a drawer?

Like melting wax, that costly alabaster,
Savons de Provence, a stab of jasmine,
With always the dark undertone of cedar.

Flesh or scented memory, which is more?
Divine perfume, three separate notes in one.
To use the gift or hoard it in a drawer,
With always the dark undertone of cedar.

3. Spider

There is a dreaded creature at the center.
To see it line you eye up with the sun,
But watch your step, you could become a spider.

Remember how your grandmother embroidered,
Lost within a web of concentration?
There is a dreaded creature at the center.

Radii and circles sketched on air.
Walk the wire you spin from pure adrenalin,
But watch your step, you could become a spider.

She can gouge, devour you. Beware.
Attach silk threads to objects to stay sane.
There is a dreaded creature at the center.

Go even further. Glower like an evil star,
Stroll through your creation and feel nothing,
But watch your step, you could become a spider.

Placenta, halo, two views of the sphere,
The hawk, the snake and all that lives between.
There is a dreaded creature at the center,
But watch your step, you could become a spider.

Holy Well

In Graiguenamanagh, I made a pilgrimage today.
The path I followed was an arrow
shooting through high grass.
I was the slug who passed by every blade.

I walked a lonely stretch
of wide, smooth river to Saint Mullin's, flowing
and yet staying
between leafy banks, accepting
their embrace, flooding
when there is no
other choice,

unlike the ocean
flooding twice a day,
erasing our incriminating prints.

This way along the Barrow
makes your foot soles not
your own. That blister
hobbles every sinner
who has come before you.

Other eyes have witnessed
yellow iris gild an emerald meadow,
a white pony stare from river tawny depths,
a driftwood heron stuck on the lip of a eel weir
(white tumult around grey stasis),
fishermen who've slipped
off the hook of time,

cloistered and yet free
to accept the plainsong of a blackbird,
orisons of wild roses,
moths flitting through their breviaries,
the monotony of an eternity
of green, the leg over leg, page
after page, hauling of the body
up that tow path, all the time anticipating
coming back depleted, flat, the chapters
closing with the wrack and pinion
masterly mechanics of a lock.

I stop
like a wound down clock,
just stop, let time walk on without me.

Look down, look up, observe
the river, how it moves
fast and slow within itself, staying
level even as it curves

past the lures
of the world on the bank,
a parking lot, flash cars and beer cans,
a mc-mansion on a hillside like a star,
a pastel village melting fast as ice cream in the heat,

This is where we two
must part. You will continue
ever more peacefully downhill
to the sea, while I
will struggle up the steep slope
of the home stretch, stand

in the nave of the great monastic ruin
kept erect by ivy,
a skeleton by wire.

As well to keep the rain
from falling, dead
from rising, old teeth
ripped out of a wavy
graveyard, bones
processing to the end
and source of all the fuss,
a tiny cress and fern fringed pool,
a child's brimming face,
a daisy bearing spring water
in a basin to the sun.

Potable and cool.
I drink it from my palms, drink
my fill, not knowing
I'd been parched for so long,
centuries really.